Etsy

The Ultimate Guide Made Simple for Entrepreneurs to Start Their Handmade Business and Grow To an Etsy Empire

If you're interested in learning more ways to start or expand your business, I've added a preview of another book of mine at the end of this book about **Dropshipping**: *The Ultimate Dropshipping BLUEPRINT Made Simple - Find, Launch, And Sell Your First Private-Label Product*

Check out the whole book and others written by me on Amazon.com

Introduction

Do you like making handmade items that reflect your artistic, whimsical, or romantic side? Or perhaps, you just love going antiquing and raiding your grandparent's old trunk and cupboards? Then Etsy should be the place for you.

For a long time now, Etsy has become the go-to online marketplace for artisans who want to get their pieces out into the market or for hobbyists who want to earn a little extra. And if you have a great product, some business savvy, and good marketing intuition, then you're sure to find a niche in Etsy.

The competition is tough, but this book is going to help you gain success on Etsy. Here, you'll find all the basic information you need to start your own shop, create a strong brand, and catch shoppers' attention. You will find tips on how to make the best of your item listings, descriptions, and titles, as well as how to take great pictures that really show off your items.

Having trouble with the math? Don't worry! This book also has that covered. You will find simple and easy guides that will help you get the right price and ensure that you get the profits you deserve!

Go through this book and create your own Etsy empire!

Table of Contents

Introduction i

Chapter 1: All About Etsy 1

    The Etsy Business Model...1

    Navigating Etsy 2

    Etsy's Popularity...4

Chapter 2: Your Product 6

    Developing your Product Brand...6

    Getting the sales going 7

Chapter 3: Etsy's Do's And Don'ts 10

    Uniquely Etsy... 10

    Un-Listables 13

    Penalties for rule breakers... 14

Chapter 4: Setting up shop 16

    Personalized Experience 16

    Banners 17

    The Text: Shop Titles and Shop Announcements 17

    Arranging The Sections 18

    Your Profile.. 18

Chapter 5: Setting up Policies and Correct Pricing................. 22

    Policies in general... 22

    Correct and Fair Pricing 25

Chapter 6: Making Sales 28

    Taking bankable pictures... 28

    Taking 'professional' photos 28

    Directing traffic (SEO optimization) 32

Conclusion 35

Chapter 1:

All About Etsy

For everyone who has a love of handmade, original, and vintage crafts, Etsy is certainly the place to be. It is the biggest and most popular place to buy and sell handmade crafts and supplies, giving creators, artists, and entrepreneurs a place to start off their businesses with little hassle and a big marketplace. In Etsy, There are plenty of opportunities for anyone who wants to start a small business.

The Etsy Business Model

In order for you to fully grasp what Etsy and how you can make a living off of Etsy, you also need to understand what Etsy's business model is and how it makes money.

First of all, Etsy is not the same as eBay, although there are similar concepts. People tend to equate the two because a lot of people make many of their purchases from both sites, but there are fundamental differences.

Anything goes on eBay, but Etsy tends to have certain rules. All in all, Etsy claims that it aims to allow sellers and buyers to get reconnected with each other and give people a venue to buy and support independent artists, and small business entrepreneurs.

So how does Etsy make money? Etsy charges sellers a small fee for each item they display on the site, and they also collect a commission for every item sold, all of which are assessed at the end of the month. These fees can be paid for through a credit card or through a PayPal account.

Navigating Etsy

Registration

Anyone can look around the Etsy site and see the listed crafts on the site, but if you're intent on buying or becoming part of the Etsy community, you will have to register. Registration is free and easy and no more complicated than most other sites. All they ask for is an E-mail address, user name and password. They don't even ask for a credit card number at this point.

But if you intend to put up your craft on sale, you will need to upgrade to a seller account. This will require a major credit card such as Visa, MasterCard, or American Express, as well as your shipping and billing address.

Once you've created an account, Etsy will send you a confirmation e-mail. Make sure to check your junk and spam folder if it doesn't show up in your inbox. Once you click the link, Etsy will send you a second email welcoming you to the site.

Tips:

- Don't disregard the importance of the user name and password. Keep in mind that your user name ends up being your shop name as well and the only way you can change your shop name is by making another account. This means having to move all your items manually and having to pay another set of fees, not to mention losing the brand recognition you've been working hard to achieve. Worst of all is that you lose track of all the conversations, customer feedback, and sales records you had in the previous shop as these can't be moved to the new one, so it's probably best if you start with a really well thought out user name.

- Make sure that your password is at least 6-8 characters long and try to add some numbers and symbols in there. Don't use birthdays or anything personal that someone can easily look up. Instead, use something creative and meaningful to you alone.

- Etsy won't allow the use of profane or racist words in the username so don't even think about it! And just to be safe, don't use any trademarked words in your username.

Through the website

The homepage of any site is often where you'll find yourself returning to again and again, which is why it's important for you to understand what features Etsy's homepage offers.

The homepage gives you easy access to the numerous on-site features such as Links, Categories, Handpicked Items, Ways to Shop, Etsy Finds, Featured Seller, Blog posts and Recently listed Items.

Keep in mind that there will be fewer selections if you aren't signed in.

- The links featured at the top of the homepage make the Etsy site easy to navigate. The links let you shop, sell, gain access to community activities and the Etsy blog, also called Storque, with great posts about all things handmade. You will also find the 'Help' button among the links. If you are signed up to your account, you will also find the link to access your account, or sign out.

- Buyers have a lot of features available to them, such as the Pounce tool which lets a buyer see the listings of undiscovered sellers and the Time machine page, which allows buyers to see newly listed items, those that are expiring, and those that have been sold recently.

- The header bar gives you access to your feed, conversations, favorites and, of course, your shop. This is where the Etsy logo is, which brings you back to the homepage wherever you may be in the site, as well as links for registration and signing in (if you haven't yet). From the header bar, you can also find the links for Handmade and Vintage Items listed on the site, as well as craft supplies and other shops.

- To help buyers browse through the millions of items listed on Etsy, categories are listed. In fact, the items on sale are organized into 31 categories, such as accessories, clothing, bags, wood work, etc.

- The handpicked items featured on Etsy's homepage features items that other Etsy users have placed in the treasury list, which were then picked up by Etsy staffers and . These are often chosen according to a certain theme such as color, design, or a special holiday and can change frequently.

Tip: A good way to learn more about how others became successful on Etsy is reading up on the Featured Seller that Etsy features every few days.

Your Account

Your account gives you access to all the info you might need. It lets you keep track of your purchases, see the feedback you get from costumers, your profile, your Etsy bill, your billing and shipping info, and any apps you might be using that are related to Etsy.

Your account also has links that are very useful for new sellers, such as the Seller Handbook that has all the articles you need to know about selling on Etsy. Here, you will also find the App gallery, which features Etsy related apps that can help you manage your store, as well as all the necessary links to manage your online shop, such as your listings, options for deleting or renewing items on sale, and rearranging featured listings.

Etsy's Popularity

One of the best ways to become a good seller is by figuring out the buyer and knowing why people like shopping at Etsy.com so much.

- One of the things that shoppers love about Etsy is how easy it is for them to find, unique and high-quality items. There are thousands of handcrafted and vintage items listed on Etsy that can't be found anywhere else.

- The sheer extent of items listed on Etsy already means you're pretty sure to find what you're looking for. They have accessories, woodworks, ceramics, jewelry, metal craft and so much more. There's so much to choose from.

- It's the place to be if you're looking for craft supplies. The supplies category on Etsy already has close to a million items, ranging from fabrics to stamps, from beads to buttons.

- There are also those who, aside from enjoying the shopping experience they have at Etsy, like the fact that they are handing their money directly to the artists. This means that every purchase actually heads straight to the maker without any middlemen, which also means the items are often priced very reasonably.

All in all, the Etsy admin has done their best to make it easy to navigate the website and set up shop. If worse comes to worse, you can always ask for help from staffers if you need it, just make sure that you understand the terms and policies.

Chapter 2:

Your Product

If you want to start an online business through Etsy, there are a lot of considerations. One of the most important factors are the products you will be selling after all those are what you're whole business is based on? Whether you're a professional craftsman looking to earn extra or if you're a stay at home parent aiming to turn your hobby into a small business, you have to make sure that what you're creating is something you're proud to sell.

Developing your Product Brand

There are millions of online shoppers in Etsy, just as there are millions of items listed on the site, which means you need to find a way to catch shoppers' attention and make them want to buy your product. You have to make your items stand out

Making it special

As mentioned above, one of the reasons why Etsy is so popular is because the products are often one of a kind and hold special meaning to the buyer. Successful artisans are often the ones who create items that hold deeper meaning and make buyers think, or the designs and items trigger nostalgia, romance or positive emotions. These items often have motivational, inspirational, or spiritual messages or have symbols, figures, or taglines derived from pop culture which makes them special or personal to the buyer. Having a product that speaks to many people or is "relatable" is a big leg-up for any aspiring online entrepreneur.

Tip: Spy on the competition. One of the best ways to get some great insight on the market and how to present your brand is by taking a look at some of the more successful sellers. Take a look at their products and try to see what makes it special and why many people are buying. If you happen to fall in the same category, try to take a look at what makes your product different from theirs and what other feature you can add to make your product pop.

Showcasing your prime product

Choosing a prime product is important because it sets the mood for your whole store. This product should be your favorite to do as well as your favorite finished product and should be something that embodies the core of your business. You have to choose the best that you can make and build your business around it. Of course, as you grow, learn, and experiment as an artist, your business will grow and evolve too, and you can always change your prime product when you feel that your art and your business have evolved.

Getting the sales going

A little is good, but more is better

To be able to live on your online business, you will need to have consistent sales, and this means having a lot of products on your listings. A lot of Etsy sellers will tell you that business grows as you expand your listing, and most have found that there is a significant increase in sales once you reach 120 items listed on the site.

Having more products means more options for buyers, more tags, more traffic and more sales. You will have some regular shoppers who will make up a bulk of what your online transactions amount to, but new products will also attract new shoppers. Remember to stay in a certain set of categories that are connected with each other, such as shoes, clothing, bags, and accessories. Having a seemingly random listing will confuse shoppers and might put them off, for example, if you're known for selling vintage clothing, suddenly selling antique woks might not be a good idea.

Make them Match

Making products that come as a set or match together is a great idea. Making coordinated items that look great together is like inviting your customers to buy more than one item or encouraging them to come back for more once they receive the item and love the quality.

Also, you can offer discounts for customers buying sets or collections, especially if you find some of your products are starting to gather dust.

Staying ahead

There are so many online trends nowadays that just take off out of nowhere. Overnight successes aren't new and they happen almost every day. If you want to be a successful Etsy seller, you have to keep an eye out on the trends, Keep an eye on top selling products on the Etsy homepage and change or adapt according to what you think is popular. The blog page linked on Etsy's homepage can also give you some insight on which colors, styles, and gift ideas are most popular. The trending page will show which designs and patterns are currently selling and is also worth checking out.

Also, keep an eye on YOUR top selling items. If you find that a certain item is selling better, then you can think of ways to expand that line. For example, if your handcrafted sea-shell bracelets are doing well, then maybe you can add sea-shell necklaces or rings as well, or if your pink handcrafted wallets are doing well, then think of expanding in different colors. Remember that the more options you provide, the more sales you're likely to make.

Do your homework: market research

Creating products that you love is a blessing unto itself, but making a living off of it involves a bit more. You need intuition and good sense if you hope to make good money in online sales, which is why it is so important that you know your target demographic and what they really want. You have to turn the product that you love creating into something that people will love to buy as well.

You can use social media sites such as Facebook, Twitter, and Pinterest for your new products. You can post pictures of your products and, if you already have a shop, include links that lead to your Etsy account. By doing this, you will also get some feedback about your product or concept and you'll be able to gauge how good your idea sounds to others. A good seller should listen to feedback and values interactions with the customer.

Tips:

- Keep an eye out on which products gives you the biggest margin of profit and expand on that line.

- Try to become an expert on what you do. Remember that if you're good at creating something, then there are those who are already great at it. Keep honing and improving your craft so that you can grow and expand with the market.

- If you want to protect your creative product, then you can register your unique designs. All the information and registration forms needed to apply for copyright from the U.S. Copyright office can be found on the net from the government website.

Don't get discouraged when you find that the creations you love so much aren't really selling yet. Remember that you're no longer creating for yourself but for other people who might have different tastes than you personally. If you find that your creations aren't catching on, try making them in varied designs or colors and keep your target market in mind.

Chapter 3:

Etsy's Do's And Don'ts

Now it's time to get down to Etsy business. This chapter will be all about setting up your Etsy shop. Here, you will learn what you can and can't sell, what you can do to make your shop really stand out, a method for appropriate pricing, and the Etsy policies you have to follow.

Uniquely Etsy

As mentioned before, a lot of people associate Etsy with eBay, except that it's for handmade and vintage items, and indeed the two are the same in essence. They are both sites where people can buy and sell items in exchange for paying listing fees, and they also include member feedback as a rating system for sellers. But there are plenty of technical differences that are important to note as well.

- Firstly, Etsy doesn't use the auction format that Ebay does. In Etsy, you put up a price, and that's that.

- Although Etsy is getting there, it's got a long way to go in catching up with eBay when it comes to sheer community size and doesn't have eBay's breadth of items.

- The biggest difference, however, is that, unlike eBay, where you can sell almost anything there is, Etsy limits the sellers on what they can sell. A seller has to meet rather strict criteria in order to set up a shop.

10

List-ables

Basically, there are three kinds of items that you can sell on Etsy, vintage, handmade, and craft supplies. This may seem limited but these are very general, and you'll be surprised at the amount of items that can be found on this site.

Of course, there are certain items that can be considered as part of each category, you may have some vintage, craft supplies, or a handmade item made of vintage material. All you have to do is choose which category your item belongs. Try to get into a buyer's head and find out which category your demographic would most likely look through first.

Handmade Items

The main reason Etsy came into being was to provide an alternative market place for handcrafted items. This is something that is very important to them and is included in their mission statement. They want a marketplace for artisans to sell THEIR crafts. This means no mass produced or commercial items. And you also can't sell anything on Etsy that someone else made, even if it is handmade.

Defining 'Handmade' according to Etsy

Of course, when you say handmade, there are plenty of possible interpretations, so here are some specifics:

- Altering or improving pre-existing items, or upcycling. Turning something mass produced into new, more creative, and better quality items is still handmade in Etsy's book. If you like cutting up old jeans and turning them into short with beads and ribbons, or screen-printing designs you made into shirts, then you're still good to go, as long as the alterations and improvements are made by hand. However, it's important to remember that Etsy will check your items and if they don't think that you've altered it enough, or that you simply repaired or tailored it, then your item might not fit the criteria.

- Packaging doesn't count. Just repackaging commercial products is a no-no. Etsy won't consider store bought bath soaps in a nice, artisan basket as handmade.

- 'Handmade' kits. Ready to assemble items that you "handmade" do not fit Etsy's criteria, unless you just use the material and change much of the design and make it really your own.

- Getting assistance. Etsy recognizes that sometimes you need more than just one pair of hands to make your artwork or manage your shop. As long as it's just assistance, such as someone who helps you sew, or someone who helps in printing, then you're good. An assistant to help manage your shop is also allowed. As long as you still do majority of the production of the items, then you're alright.

Vintage Items

Etsy is also a great place for those who love the classic. You can find all sorts of collectibles and vintage goods. From books to shoes, to toys, if you're looking for vintage, you're sure to find it at Etsy.

How old is vintage?

In order for your items to be considered vintage, they have to be at least 20 years old. If your item doesn't fit this criterion, then you can either wait for it to become vintage, or think of some other way of making use of it.

Supplies

Etsy allows sellers of craft supplies to list on site, even if they are commercial craft supplies. This is actually a way for Etsy to support the artisan community it has on site. This way, the artisans selling on Etsy don't have to look elsewhere when looking for the supplies the need for their items.

Supplies such as buttons, paper, beads, tools, fabric, threads, feathers, and so much more can also be sold on Etsy.

However, supplies that can be considered ready for use, even if they are also classified as commercial crafting supplies, are not allowed. Mass produced items that can be used with handmade items but aren't considered craft supplies are not allowed either. Examples include makeup brushes and the like.

Un-Listables

Again, to reiterate, anything mass produced, anything someone else made, and anything you think might be "vintage" but is less than 20 years old is not allowed on Etsy. But there are some other considerations that need clarification as it's important that you know what items might not be allowed on the site.

You might think that anything that anything that fits into one of the aforementioned categories are okay to sell on Etsy, but there are further prohibitions. There are certain products that may fit one or more of the categories but are still not allowed to be listed on the site:

- Guns and weapons

- Alcoholic beverages

- Drugs and any paraphernalia associated with drugs

- Animals and illegal animal products

- Motor vehicles such as cars, motorcycles, etc.

- Tobacco related products

- Any form of pornography

- Real estate

- Anything that Etsy deems to be promoting racism, sexism, or any other kind of prejudice based on other person's religion, ethnicity or social status. Basically, products that promote hate or intolerance.

- Anything Etsy deems to be glorifying illegal or violent acts

Mature content

Although pornography is a strict no-no in Etsy, they do allow items under the NC-17 classification, which means items that contain depictions of male and female sexual organs, actual sexual activity, and depictions of violent or graphic scenes are still allowed. There are certain rules you have to follow in listing items like these though, and it would be best to follow them to the letter.

Etsy wants to ensure that the listings still remain appropriate for all ages. This means that items that have mature content have to be tagged as mature content and that the word mature should be included in the title. This way, users can keep such items from popping up by adding 'no mature' when they search for items. Secondly, items that have depictions of sexual or violent acts must have an audience appropriate picture as a thumbnail. Pictures that show the whole item are allowed to be included as long as they aren't the thumbnail that pops up when doing a search or if the item shows up on someone's feed.

Selling Services

Being an online marketplace for goods, Etsy doesn't generally have room for selling services such as dog walking, house sitting, or massages. Even services that may be needed by fellow members such as tailoring and restorations are not allowed on the listings.

HOWEVER, if you offer a service that then leads to the creation of a new and actual item, such as offering your services as a logo or graphic designer, then you're good to go. Also, offering workshops is allowed as long as you give the participants a real and tangible object such as a booklet or a sample product afterwards.

Penalties for rule breakers

So what happens if you happen to break some rules? Your item can get flagged by staffers or other members so that your item can be reviewed by Etsy. This will all be anonymous, and you can flag items that you think are inappropriate, as well.

If it really does violate Etsy's rules, then the item will likely be taken off the listing. Most of the time, Etsy will notify you and ask you to remove the prohibited item, or add the needed tags, etc. If you don't comply, then Etsy staff will remove the item themselves. If you commit an extreme offense, your selling privileges may be suspended or even terminated. It's worth noting that you will still have to pay any outstanding fees if your listed item is delisted or your account gets terminated.

Etsy is a place of opportunity and lofty principles, and you can make good use of this if you know what you are allowed and not allowed to do on the site. Remember that Etsy is still a community and you need to build up a reputation, which is why it's so important to keep your nose clean and have a clear grasp of community rules.

Chapter 4:

Setting up shop

Your Etsy shop, as it is when you first create it, will be very plain and almost empty. But look at it this way, this gives you such a great opportunity to personalize and jazz up your shop. Etsy gives you the freedom to personalize your shop, and you can add a banner, choose an avatar, and use sections to organize your goods and make the shop seem more YOU than just a blank page.

Personalized Experience

As mentioned in the preceding chapters, the Etsy experience is all about shoppers getting closer to the actual creators of the art. If you want to invite more buyers to get into your shop and buy your items, you have to make it stand out and personalize the shop as much as you can. You want the shop to be a reflection of you and your product.

You can make your shop unique and personalized by choosing custom banners, colors, and fonts, as well as other visuals. Also, the text that you choose to add has to be consistent with this as well. If Etsy shoppers feel connected to you or relate to you on a personal level, then you can look forward to bigger sales.

Tip: Make sure your grammar and spelling are tight. You don't want to be seen as a sloppy shop keeper. Having spelling or grammatical errors on your shop tile or announcements can make potential buyers think twice of availing any of your items.

Banners

The banner is the graphic that goes across the top of your shop page. You can create a banner from scratch easily using common programs. Make sure that the banner sets the mood for your shop correctly and helps you create the aesthetic you want to achieve.

And don't worry too much; you can change the banner whenever you want. You might want to change the banner to promote certain discounts or change it according to special holidays or trending colors or designs, etc.

Making Banners

There is a lot of free software that you can use to create your banners. Well known photo editing apps such as Photoshop, GIMP, Picnik and the like can help do the job. If you're on a PC, the tried and tested paint program can help you create your banner.

Don't forget that if you're not into the making-digital-banners thing, then you can always have professionals do this for you. Remember how Etsy lets you offer services as long as it results in a new and tangible product? Well, an example would be your shop's banner.

Once you're done, all you have to do is upload your banner in the Info and Appearance section under the Shop Settings button, and Etsy will upload the chosen JPEG image file.

To check how your banner looks, simply click on the Shop icon that's found on the header bar.

The Text: Shop Titles and Shop Announcements

The shop title and announcements are a great way for you to give any potential visitors a heads up on what your shop offers.

Here are a few factors to consider in making sure that you've come up with the best shop title and announcement you can make:

1. The shop title should be considered as a kind of slogan for your shop. This short sentence or phrase should sum up what your shop is about. If you happen to be selling zany and quirky items, make sure your title fits the bill. It probably wouldn't do to have a serious slogan when you're selling fun or wacky items.

2. On the other hand, you can use the shop announcement section to call attention to the types of items your selling, or sales and discounts that you have in the coming days. Another good use for the shop announcement section is for when you tend to sell pricier items. You can use the shop announcement as a way to explain why your pieces are worth the price. For example, if you happen to use expensive materials or the work you do is very intricate.

Take note that your shop announcement's first 160 characters as well as the shop title will make up the description for your shop. You'll find the text boxes for your shop title and shop announcement by clicking the Info and Appearance link under the Shop Settings button.

Arranging The Sections

How you arrange your shop has a big effect on your sales. In fact, every store, whether digital or physical, have to arrange and systematize the placement of their items to make it easier for potential buyers to find anything they need or maybe even spot something awesome that they didn't intend on buying in the first place. You have to make it easy for your customers to navigate your shop and find the goods they came to buy.

Etsy gives you the freedom to organize your goods. This is especially helpful if you sell many different yet related items, such as pens, notebooks, and paper. But even if you only sell one kind of item, such as jewelry, you still have to organize the sections so that it becomes easier for your customers to find the kind that they want. You can choose to organize them according to size, price, pattern or color.

All in, Etsy allows you to have ten sections plus the default sections called All items that can be found in every shop. Again, the links for creating your shop's sections are also found in the Info and Appearance link under Shop Settings.

Your Profile

The profile you put up on Etsy is one of the ways that your customers can get to know you and get a sense of who you are. By reading your profile, your customers might feel a connection and feel that they can relate to you. This is always a good thing since one of Etsy draws is that it makes the customer feel closer to the people who create their goods.

Your profile is where you upload a picture, which is also called an avatar. As expected, this section will include your name, address, birthday, and gender (or not, it's up to you), your bio and the date when you joined Etsy. If you happen to have an actual, physical shop, typing it out on Etsy will allow customers to find your shop through the Shop Local tool provided on the website. You can also add as many as 14 of the materials that you love to use.

The Avatar

Your avatar or profile picture is the image that will be representing you ad your shop. It will be your avatar that appears in your posts, comment, or participate in the Etsy community. You have to make sure that you choose an avatar that truly represents you and your shop.

When choosing an avatar, you might consider using your logo for the store to reinforce branding. Even you don't have a logo yet, or if you just happen to really love your product, then you can choose a picture of your prime product as an avatar. You can even just post a picture of yourself, but try to add your products in there so that, at some point, you're still showing off what your shop has to offer.

Keep in mind that the picture is really small and if the picture you choose is too big, then it might appear distorted.

The bio

A lot of people can feel squeamish about saying and, most of all, writing about themselves, but making a first-rate bio is essential if you want to have a successful Etsy shop.

Here are a few reasons why the bio has to be well thought out:

- Your bio is one of the best ways for your customers to get to know you as a seller. Keep in mind that this is one of Etsy's biggest draws.

- This is where you can bring any accomplishments regarding your work to light. You might have had a piece at a gallery, or maybe you won an award for your work. Mentioning this on your bio makes sure that everyone who visits your shop can find out about your accomplishments.

Writing an eye-catching bio

When you're writing your bio, don't expect that you'll get it perfect at the first draft. Remember to read your work over again after you've rested a bit so that you can be sure that what you've written sound right to your ears.

Here are some things to remember when writing your Etsy shop bio:

- Remember that the tone of your bio should be welcoming and approachable. Say hello, and welcome all the possible visitors to your shop. And don't forget to thank them for coming by.

- Try to make your first paragraph fun and upbeat, you want the very first paragraph to be attention grabbing and interesting. By doing so, you will be making the visitors to your shop more inclined to keep reading your bio and check out the items you have at your shop.

- Try to include funny or touching anecdotes about how your store was started or about your personal journey that brought you to Etsy.

- Make your bio more readable, meaning that you should keep it short and easy to understand. Don't include long sentences or paragraphs, as this can turn people off from reading your bio to the end. Cut your writing up into shorter, to the point paragraphs.

- If you want to really catch people's eye and if it fits in with your shop, for example, you sell whimsical unicorn jewelry, then you can opt to add some spice by writing a fictional bio that sets the mood for your shop.

- Read your work over! You need to proofread and check spelling and grammar just to be sure that everything looks polished and professional.

Tip:

Be wise about the words you use in your shop title, shop announcement, and shop sections as those are the words that Google and other search engines, as well as Etsy's own search bar, use when people search for items. Clever and funny wordings are great, but if you want to show up in the search engines then try to make a straightforward description and make sure that the key words are mentioned more than once. This is part of SEO which you should also look into as it can greatly increase your hit-count.

Chapter 5:

Setting up Policies and Correct Pricing

Although Etsy already has their policies regarding sellers and buyers, you have to make a set of policies for your shop in particular. You want to make some ground rules for your buyers to follow as well as policies regarding returns, exchanges, shipping, and payments.

Making rules and shop policies can save you a lot of headaches when it comes to your transactions. You won't end up arguing with clients because you already have policies regarding every aspect of the transaction. Of course, your policies aren't set in stone, and you can add more along the way when you find certain misunderstandings always popping up.

Policies in general

Although you have the freedom to make your own unique policies, don't forget that you're still covered by Etsy's overall store policies. Remember to make sure that your policies aren't one-sided. Customers won't be very willing to do business with you if they feel like your policies are unfair or out them in a vulnerable spot. Remember to protect your business as well as your customer. Also, make sure that your policies are simple and easy to understand.

Money Matters: Making Payment Policies

When you consider payment policies you are basically ensuring that you get paid, how you get paid, how you'll pay for taxes. Etsy does its best to make this simple but money matters can still seem daunting to many people, but nonetheless, it is an important part of ensuring you run a tight ship.

Payment options

When determining payment policies, you also have the option of choosing what payment method you're willing to accept. You can opt to go purely digital, or you can allow for direct payment or personal checks.

The most popular payment method currently on Etsy is PayPal. It's fast, easy, and you get paid instantly. PayPal also has protection clauses for both buyers and sellers. If you happen not to have a PayPal account, it's also easy to register -- all you need is major credit or debit card. You might want to upgrade to a Business account, though, that is you want buyers to be able to pay through credit cards.

Although the world is deep into the digital age, there are still certain people who distrust online transaction and prefer paying with money order or personal checks. The only problem here is that you won't get payment immediately, and you'll have to wait for the money order or check to be delivered.

Tip: If you choose to accept money order or checks as payment, make sure that the checks clear before sending your customer the items they ordered, just to be safe.

You can also accept other forms of payment that aren't monetary such as, say, silk neckties or what have you. You just have to make sure you specify this in your store policies page. You can change all of this on the shop settings sections of your account page. Keep in mind that these setting will hold true for all of your

The sales tax

This is one of the things that artists just don't want to get into, but you don't have to do it alone. When you start a business, you want to make sure that it's all above board, and this means you want to be solid when it comes to paying your taxes and whatnot. You will want to consult a lawyer or an accountant just to make sure you have a clear grasp of the tax laws in your state, or, if you don't want to get into that, then just read up on those laws yourself.

Once you've determined that you need to pay sales taxes, Etsy makes it easy with their tax calculator that lets you collect taxes during the checkout process. Etsy will then assess the sales tax for your buyer wherever they may be.

You do have to set up Etsy's tax calculator, but the steps are fairly easy. You just have to enter the region you're in as well as the state's tax rate. You can also add taxes on shipping fees if the law requires it. All of these can be found in the Sales Tax Settings page in the shipping and payment link under shop settings.

Choosing your preferred currency

Although most of the sellers on Etsy are American citizens, there are still many others who live elsewhere, on the other hand, there are some stores that have a majority of their clients from other places. This is why Etsy offers the option of choosing a preferred currency. You can convert the currencies and even opt to have the amount rounded up under the Price Conversion Preference by clicking Round Prices.

The preferred currency option can also be found on the Shipping and Payment link, under Shop Settings.

Shipping policy

It's important that you present potential customers with a clear enumeration of your shipping policy so that they can have their mind at rest when it comes to when their package arrives or what delivery service you will be using. You have to state what shipping service you intend to use, what type of delivery you mail your items if you ship internationally, and if you include tracking or insurance with your deliveries. It is also important to note when you deliver items after they have been ordered. This can vary, especially if you custom make artwork for every buyer.

Tip: A great way to increase sales is by offering discounts if the customer is purchasing more than one item.

Other specifics you may want to include in your shipping policy include whether you're willing to rush certain orders in exchange for extra fees and how you intend to package the items.

Regarding returns and exchanges

No matter how great your items are, there will always be some that find their way back to you. Whether they got broken on the way, or they weren't what the customer wanted, or maybe, due to your booming business, you mistakenly sent the wrong item.

What should your return and exchange policy cover?

- Whether you allow for returns and exchanges, and regarding which items. There are certain items that aren't really okay to return or exchange, such as bathing suits, underwear, and personal hygiene products.

- What kind of circumstances do you allow for returns and exchanges? You have to state when you are willing to accept returns or exchanges, like when the product was damaged upon shipping or if you sent the wrong item. You also have to state when you won't allow it, for example, if it was broken upon handling by the client or if they ordered the wrong size despite the size chart you already posted.

- You have to set the amount of time your customers have to exchange or return an item as well as who will pay for the extra set of shipping fees.

Once you've determined all these important aspects, you can post them on the Shop Policies Page that is already included in your Etsy shop. Don't forget to greet and welcome your customers in your policy page.

Correct and Fair Pricing

Now it's time to put a price on your work. This may be difficult to do, especially since you aren't exactly unbiased when it comes to your own artwork or the thrill of making your sale. But there are certain 'mathematical' ways that you can price your work so that nobody ends up feeling cheated.

Finding the right price

Over or underpricing are common errors that first-time business owners can make, and both have very negative implications. If you over price your product, you won't be able to sell that much and, no matter how good your products actually are, the sheer expense may cause them to stay on the shelves and gather dust.

On the other hand, underpricing can make you lose money, even if you do manage to sell a lot of items. Also, underpricing can make your items seem cheap.

You need to find the right price that allows you to make a healthy profit and doesn't put off potential buyers.

So how do you make sure that you have the right price? You have to add up all your expenditures in creating your piece. There's the cost of materials, the cost of your labor, as well as the recurring costs you have for your business, otherwise known as overhead.

Calculations:

To calculate the cost of materials for each piece, you have to add up all the materials and then divide them by how much you use up for each piece. If you make little purses, and two yards of cloth makes five purses for 3 dollars a yard, for $6 total, then you divide the $6 you spend on the cloth by five purses = $1.2. Calculate all other materials, such as zippers, twine, buttons, etc. in the same way.

When calculating your labor cost, add up all the hours in a day that you spend designing, creating, and marketing your product, as well as the time you spend on shipping and packaging. The best you can do is set an hourly rate for yourself. Take note that you will be giving yourself a bit less when you're just starting. Once you've figured on an hourly rate, come up with a solid number of items that you can create, market and ship. For example, if you spend 3 hours designing and creating 20 pieces of pendants, and you spend an hour photographing and marketing all of them, you spend 4 hours of work on 20 pendants. If you plan on paying yourself $15 per pendant, that's $60 divided by 20 pendants, your labor cost per pendant will be $3.

The same process comes when calculating your overhead, which is made up of all your equipment, tools, rent, etc. This includes office supplies, tools you use, your internet and electric, as well as Etsy and PayPal fees.

Add all this up and then double it and that will be your wholesale price. The extra, doubled money will be your profit and the money you will be able to use to invest into your business. For example, if you calculate that all the expenses, added up, total $11, the wholesale price would be $22, and as retail, you have to multiply again, times two which makes it around $40. Now this is just the usual way of calculating, if you want to multiply it by 3 or 1.5, then that's up to you.

Tip: It is always important that you have separate retail and wholesale prices. First of all, you want to make it more attractive for customers to buy in bulk when you have a cheaper wholesale price. Also, you will want to make it possible for yourself to have a sales or discounts for special occasions, and you don't want to be losing your profits when you do.

Keep your demographic in mind and how much they can actually afford. If you think that you're items are a little too expensive for your target market, then try to sell cheaper items by adjusting the type of material you use or by using a simpler design. Don't forget to specify in the descriptions why some items are pricier, just so that your customers know what they're paying for.

Chapter 6:

Making Sales

Now that you have your account, your shop, and your policies ready, you have to make sure that you actually make sales. This all starts with posting beautiful pictures of your items, coming up with engaging titles, and the actual selling process.

Taking bankable pictures

One of the biggest factors when it comes to selling stuff online is taking attractive pictures. Your customers won't be able to pick up your item and scrutinize every detail, so you have to take pictures that will make them want to buy your items.

Tip:

- You don't really have to spend too much money on a camera. Sometimes it's all about placement etc. and you can also just download photo editing apps to adjust your pictures. It is important, however, that you know what your camera has to offer and that you pay for features that you actually need, such as a macro-setting (for extremely close close-ups) and autofocus.

Taking 'professional' photos

This doesn't really mean that you have to hire a professional to take photos of your items; your photos just have to LOOK professional. This means making sure the item itself isn't blurred, the background isn't messy, and that you have ample lighting. Of course, there are photo editing apps that can make your pictures brighter, but it is generally better if your photos don't look too edited. That way, you don't misrepresent an item.

Using backgrounds

You want to have a simple, even blurred out background so that it directs focus to your item, Most Etsy sellers choose plain white backgrounds which offer great contrast to their items, whatever the color may be.

But if you're feeling a little bored with a plain white background, or you think your item would look better with a more creative background then you can definitely do that. For example, if you sell gardening tools, you might like to take pictures with gardening soil or green grass as a background. Anything can work, such as wood surfaces, tiles, cobblestones, etc.

Tips:

- Make sure the background isn't too busy. Having too much going on in your background can take the focus off your item, and customers might not be able to appreciate the beauty of it if it's competing with a busy pattern.

- Using a mildly reflective surface is great if you're showing off really intricate or delicate work, or if your item is of a darker color. Just make sure it doesn't shine too brightly that it actually takes attention away from your item.

- Use contrasts in color and texture. If your piece is a black, really smooth piece, then setting it on back ground with light colors and a slightly grainy texture can really make it pop.

- DON'T use a basic black background against dark pieces as your items can get lost. Instead, use something with a bit of shade, such charcoal or ebony.

- Check you pictures and make sure you don't accidentally include something you didn't want to, such as old newspapers in the back ground, or your hamper.

Smart use of props

Another way to call attention to your item is by adding some props in the pictures. Props can make the pictures more interesting as well as set a certain mood. You can use props to enhance the beauty of your piece as well as reflect your personality or that of your shop. You have to make sure that your props are a reflection of your items as well as your brand and that they don't stick out like a sore thumb. For example, if you sell vintage items, setting up shiny, plastic props might end up looking awkward.

Tips:

- If you want to show your items to scale, you can use a prop that everyone can recognize and place it near your piece to show the size. An example would be a chair, a plate, a book, or a pen.

- Putting your item in its "natural" environment would also add a certain charm and interest to your pictures. For example, if you happen to be selling a pen, you can take a picture of it next to or on top of an open notebook. Remember that if it's a fun and wacky pen, use a fun and wacky notebook that accentuates it. If you happen to be selling a vintage pen, putting it next to a cheap looking notebook on a plastic table might devalue the item.

- You can place the item next to its raw materials. For example, if you sell organic, rose infused soap, you can take a picture of the finished product on top of some rose petals, or a bowl of strawberries or what have you. This is also a way of showing your customers that you use quality raw materials.

If you happen to be selling clothes or bags, it might be a good idea to add a model wearing or carrying your item. Of course you'll have to style the whole outfit to make sure the other clothes don't take the attentions away from your item or maybe, even make your item look bad.

Making headlines that POP and descriptions that simmer

Think of your item titles as headlines. They're the first thing the customer sees and they will either make them look closer, or make them turn away. You will always want the latter type of headline, but which means you have to make sure that you have a good, eye-catching title.

Even this aspect of your shops requires some artistry as you want to make your item sound as appealing as possible.

Tips:

- Use complementary words that make your item sound appealing. Instead of old, say vintage, instead of recycled say eco-friendly, instead of fixed-up use refurbished, retailored or revamped.

- Be fun and use puns, when you can. Say, if you selling fun, floral pens, you can use *Pen-tastic floral pens*, etc.

- Include some keywords that would show up in searches, such as vintage pens or eco-friendly floral purses.

- Include some basic information about the piece such as what it's made of, the color, the size, etc.

- Don't make it too long. 150 characters should be enough including spaces.

- Here are a few good examples of item titles:

    Sassy Pants: Retailored Denim Pants with Handmade Beaded Appliques

    Add some Ice: Vintage Crystal Pendants set in Brass

Descriptions hold additional information about your item. Etsy buyers want to have items that have a history or a story behind their creation, and you have to come up with an engaging story that makes your item interesting.

The description can be about the inspiration behind the items, how you started making them, or where you found or got them from (if they're vintage items).

Tips:

- Make your descriptions as personal as possible and try to tell your story as if the customer was right there beside you.

- This is where you add specifics, such as the exact size, color and material you used for the item.

  For example, using the Pen-tastic example above, your description can be:

  Do you want the stamp and smell of flowers in everything around you? Then these Pen-tastic Pens are just for you. Lovingly made and filled with lovely floral patterns, these personalized one of a kind pens add a bit of extra to you school or office bag.

  These handmade floral pens have patterns derived from nature using my own printing process at home. They are nine inches in length and have a lovely gel grip for easy handling. The ink color can be black, blue, or red, and also has a light floral scent that will remind you of gardens in bloom.

Remember that the titles and descriptions should fit the whole theme of your store. If you're going for a serious, old-timey atmosphere, then go with that and be consistent.

Directing traffic (SEO optimization)

No matter how beautiful your pictures turn out, they won't be appreciated by anyone if no one ends up visiting your shop. You will need to do everything in your power to make it easy for people to find your shop and get your items to show up when people use search engine.

This means that you have to place possible search keywords in your listing, item descriptions and titles, as well as shop announcements and shop titles. By placing keywords strategically in your item listing as well as your shop, you'll be making sure that your items will show up when people search the keywords in various search engines.

Choosing keywords

When it comes to keywords, you need to make sure you are using the best, which means that you are using keywords that people most often search for. One of the best ways that you can do this is by using tools such as Google AdWords Keyword Tool which show you how often certain keywords are used.

You'll find that the more specific key words or phrases, such as "Handmade floral Pattern pens" are searched less often than more general terms, such as "pens". But also note that the more general term often shows up with millions more of results when searched, which means there are more websites using the same keywords.

If a certain keyword is searched more often but has more results to it, then you have a big chance of going to the bottom of the pile. Your store might end up at the last pages, and most people don't check farther than the first or second page. So, this means that using keywords or phrases like "Handmade floral pattern pens" can actually make your Etsy shop page show up closer to the top and get you more visitors than simply using the word "pens" as a keyword.

Tips:

- You can also use Google AdWords Keyword Tool to check if your keywords are the best ones you can use or if there are more efficient words out there.

- Include your keywords everywhere you can, such as your item tile, description as well your shop title.

- Try to place keywords naturally. Don't overstuff your titles and descriptions. Make sure the keyword placement still sound natural and can be understood.

- You have to put your keywords in the first sentence or so. The search engine do search the whole tile or description for keywords, but the ones that the visitors read are only the first 66 characters.

Tagging

Etsy also allows you to use tags on your item listings, and Etsy uses these same tags so that shoppers can find your items besides the search tool on the site. Using strong tags can help your items to show up when anyone searches on Etsy, which is why it's so important that you use strong tags to your listings.

Again, it is important to get into your customer's head. What kind of keywords do you think they will enter when they're looking for an item very much like yours.

Tips:

- First off, add literal tags, such as "Ballpoint Pen", or simple "Pens", then add the style, "floral", "girly", "casual", "cute" or what have you. You can also add the material, color, and design motifs such as "nature", "roses", "pink" etc.

Remember that making sales is not just about a really nice picture and a good description; you also have to make a good impression on the customers that contact or start conversations with you. How you interact with your buyers is a part of building up your brand, and this is very important, considering that Etsy is all about a more personalized experience for shoppers. So make sure you put your best foot forward in conversations as well!

Conclusion

Now, you know what it takes to start a business on Etsy. It's not as simple as just having a great idea and a good product. It's about coming up with a strong brand that reflects you as a creator as well as your creations. This translates to how your shop looks, how you write your profile, how you take pictures, as well as how you present each item.

In this book, you've learned how to make a great, interesting, and eye-catching shop, how to present your items in the best light, in both a visual (photographs) and literary (descriptions) sense. You've learned the basics of Etsy, what you can and can't do, how to navigate through the site, as well as helpful policies that can make running your business easier.

You also now know how to make the needed calculations to set a good price for your items, as well as using SEO to help boost your sales. Now that you've read up on the information you need, you can start your business with surer footing.

Remember to keep the tips in mind to help give you a leg-up in all the aspects of managing your shop and selling your items. Good luck!

Finally, if you enjoyed this book, then I'd like to ask you for a favor, would you be kind enough to leave an honest review for this book on Amazon? It would help people who are looking for the same information as you to know if this is a book for them. It would be **greatly appreciated** by me as well!

Go to Amazon.com to leave a review for this book.

Thank you and good luck,
Michelle Williams

Preview of *Dropshipping*: *The Ultimate Dropshipping BLUEPRINT Made Simple - Find, Launch, And Sell Your First Private-Label Product*

Introduction

Have you ever thought of starting your own online business? If so, this book is for you. In this book, we discuss how to start selling products online through drop shipping.

In this method of doing business, you will be able to start selling products without the need to rent space for a storefront. In fact, the products no longer need to pass through you. It goes to the buyer straight from the distributor.

You can start this business in less than a thousand dollars. You can start with even less if you can do everything by yourself. In this book, we discuss the skills required to get this business off the ground and to make it successful. The information in this book is organized so that even beginners can start doing business.

We hope that the information in this book will help you start your own business. Begin reading this book and start increasing your income today!

Chapter 1

What is a Drop Shipping Business?

Drop shipping is one of the most popular ways of starting an online business. In this type of online business, you are selling products online but the products you sell never pass through you. Instead, the products you are selling goes directly from the source to the buyer.

The manufacturer creates the product. They may either store the products themselves or send it to a distributor to be sent out to people interested in the product. In normal circumstances, retailers contact the people who store the products. They order large amounts of the product and sell the products in their own stores.

Some of these distributors find that delivering directly to products users can also be profitable. They allow buyers to call them up directly and buy products from them. You can make an agreement so that the drop shipping companies will deliver to your customers.

Now that you have access to the products and a way to deliver them, you need to find ways to let people know that you are selling these products. Using various online marketing strategies, you will be able to let people know that they can have this product delivered to their homes.

If interested people see your product marketing, they may contact you or order from your store. If they complete the online purchase, you should already have their money. You should let the drop shipping company know about the purchase. Use part of their money to pay the drop shipping company. The drop shipping company then sends the product to the buyer.

For each purchase, you earn the difference between your selling price and the fees you pay the manufacturer or the distributor. The fees usually include the price of the product and the delivery and handling fees.

The profit can be a few dollars or a few hundred dollars depending on the type of product that you are selling.

Chapter 2

Finding a Profitable Product

The first challenge that you need to face when setting your first drop shipping business is finding a product that will sell.

Steps in finding a product to sell

1. Choose a niche market

All the marketing gurus will tell you to choose an industry that you are interested in. If you like sports, for example, you should look for a sports-related product. If you like fashion, you should probably choose this industry to start your drop shipping business. Start by listing the industries for which you want to start an online store. Here are some of the most popular industries online:

- Health and Wellness

- Fitness and Outdoors

- Sports

- Hobbies and crafts

- Home and kitchen products

- Tech and gadgets

- Computers and laptops

These are only some of the most popularly searched industries online all year round. You can add other industries that you have some experience with.

If you have chosen an industry, you should look for a niche in that industry that you could start a profitable business with. If you like sports, for instance, you may start by stating the specific types of sports that you know and enjoy. You could then look for certain products related to the sport that are sold by drop shipping companies.

When choosing a niche, also consider the communities that you are already connected with. Let's say you want to sell standing basketball hoops for homeowners. This is a big-ticket item in the sports and outdoor industry. It would be easier to start makings online sales if you already know where prospective buyers of the product are hangings out online. If you are considering multiple market niches, you should choose the ones where you already have access to their communities.

2. Find trending product types

You should find products with online marketing potential. To find products like these in your chosen niche, check for products related to your niche in popular e-commerce websites like Amazon. Nowadays, you can find all types of products in these websites.

It is not advisable to sell the same products you find on Amazon or any other e-commerce website. When people search for these products in the search engine, they are most likely to see Amazon pages on top of the search result page. It is almost impossible for you to beat Amazon pages in search result pages for specific product keywords.

Instead, you should look for popular product types and find alternative products for them that are not sold on Amazon and other e-commerce websites yet.

If you are planning to start selling your products in a specific area, you should also check if it is being sold in your local stores. If similar products are available in your local stores, check their prices. This will give you an idea of the amount of competition that your business will face.

Lastly, consider products that are not easily available to your target buyers. Let's say you want to start marketing the product to people in your town, you should consider if they have access to it in your local stores. If a certain product can be easily bought from these sources, they are more likely to choose the offline stores. They will only choose your online store if your store offers significantly lower prices than the competition.

3. Find product types that do not update often

When setting up online stores, it will be easier for you if there is little need for updates for the products. Some types of products like the ones in the tech industry upgrade often. Every time these products upgrade, you also need to do updates on your product pages. Choose products that do not have this problem.

4. Examine the demand for the product

When you have chosen the types of products that you are interested in selling, examine if people look for them often. Let's say you want to start selling specialized types of exercise bicycles. You noticed that they are not available in your city, and you found a certain brand that is not on Amazon yet.

Before you start looking for a supplier for that product, you should first check if there is a demand for it in the online market. You can check on Amazon for products similar to it. You could check for other brands of exercise bicycles available in Amazon. If many people are making reviews on these other brands, it is a good sign that there are many buyers for that particular product online.

Aside from checking other e-commerce websites, you should check the search volume for keywords related to the products. You can do this free by using online services like Google AdWords' Keyword Planner. You should only check the keywords that show intent to buy. Using these online services, you will be able to see how often people search for the product online.

5. Check the competing websites for your product

While checking the online demand for the product, look into the amount of competition that you would face when marketing your product. Use the keywords for the product in the search engine and check the top search results. The websites you see at the top are the ones that you will be competing with when marketing your products. If they are big names online, you should probably look for other keywords to compete with or look for other types of products.

Aside from looking at these websites up, also look into the ads that may show up in the search result pages. You will also be competing with these advertisers when marketing your product. If you are still considering multiple products to sell, you should choose the ones with the least amount of competition.

Selling other brands versus creating your own brand

In the drop shipping business, you have the option to sell already established brands. If discover a drop-shipped brand that is not yet offered anywhere online, you can choose to sell on your website. However, finding a brand that is not already available can be challenging. Almost all popular brands are already sold in popular e-commerce websites.

It is very challenging to sell such brands in the business-consumer (b2c) type products. You may be able to find some brands not offered in e-commerce stores in business-business (b2b) type products. Some brand of office equipment, for instance, cannot be found on Amazon. You could contact some of these brands and ask if they offer drop shipping to buyers.

Selling already established brands can be easier if the company is active in promoting their product. If you are the first to offer their product online, they may also offer special promotions for your online store. You need to find companies that are just starting out and support them by bringing attention to their product. You also offer them a way to promote and sell their products online without setting up their own websites.

On the other hand, you could also choose to set up your own product line in your chosen niche market. To do this, you need to start looking for manufacturers of your chosen product that do not put their own labels on the products they produce. If there are a lot of factories in your area, you may find some of these products in your own city.

If you do find a type of product that you want to add to your online store, you should start developing the packaging and branding of your product. You need a name and a branding design that fits your niche and the preferences of your target market.

Lastly, promote the said product in your online store using your own brand name. In this setup, you will be promoting not only your online store but also the product and the brand.

By selling your own brand, you will have more freedom in promoting your product. All your promotions will also help your brand. By putting all your efforts in your own product, the success of your business will depend solely on your efforts. Fewer factors will be out of your control.

Aside from this, you will also be able to control the quality of your product. If you find another manufacturer with better quality products, you can switch manufacturers. You will also be in charge of the packaging of your product. Research shows that packaging is an important basis that people use in judging the quality of a brand. Other new brands may not be as meticulous in the packaging design as you are. However, you will not be able to know how the packaging looks because you never get to see the product.

Aside from the creative license of creating your own brand, you will also have the freedom in pricing if your produce your own brand. If you sell other company's brands, you may be forced to sell on a fixed price to prevent price wars among other sellers. If you create your own brand, you will be able to price your products strategically. If there are no competitions, you may sell it at a high price. If there are too may competitions at the premium price, you could lower it to be more competitive.

Examples of drop shipped products:

You can easily create your own brand if you sell general products that can be produced in bulk by a manufacturer. Some of the earliest drop shipping entrepreneurs, for example, sold different paper sizes to offices around the country. They cold-called offices in the east coast of the United States to sell paper. These offices can then, order directly from their website. They took their product from the cheapest suppliers of paper across the country. These were then packed by a fulfillment service and delivered by an independent courier.

Later, other consumable products followed. Some sold exotic tea, while others sold whey protein to fitness enthusiasts. They merely repackaged these products and sold them as their own brands.

You can also start selling common consumable products repackaged as your own brands. However, you need to find the right manufacturers and distributors for them.

Characteristics of products that sell well online

Whenever people buy from companies they are not familiar with over the internet, they are risking their money. You need to choose the types of products that are worth taking the risk for.

Here are some of the reasons that people risk their money with new online stores:

- They are looking for specialized products

Some types of products just cannot be found in offline stores and e-commerce websites. This is the reason why you need to find niche markets that other online marketers are not familiar with. The types of products that you sell should solve unique types of problems.

- They need to see tutorials before buying

Some types of products also require special instructions to use. Because of this, people are forced to go online to look for tips on how to use the product. When they find the information they need in a website that also offers the product, they may buy from that website.

- Aim to be the exclusive distributor of a product online

One of the best ways to become successful in your drop shipping business is by becoming the exclusive distributor of a product in the online market. Most established brands would not give you this privilege. You are more likely to succeed in becoming an exclusive distributor of newer brands or products.

If you are confident that you can bring in solid sales numbers, you should also consider asking to be the exclusive distributor to a certain area. If your online store, for example, has a strong online presence in the east coast of the United States, you may have some negotiating leverage to ask to be the exclusive sales outlet of a brand in a certain area.

- Products cheaper than offline counterparts

Some people buy from new online stores because of the lower cost. Unlike brick and mortar stores, e-commerce websites do not have high overhead costs. They do not need to rent warehouses or storefronts to sell. Because of this, they may be able to offer lower prices of products. Because people are ordering in small quantities, however, the drop shipping system may have additional shipping and handling costs. You should sell products that offer good prices even with the shipping and handling fees considered.

You can check out the rest of the book on Amazon.com.

Other books written by me

(Go to Amazon.com to check these out.)

- **Penny Stocks:** *Investors Guide Made Simple – How to Find, Buy, Maximize Profits, and Minimize Losses with Penny Stock Trading*

- **Dropshipping:** *The Ultimate Dropshipping BLUEPRINT Made Simple - Find, Launch, And Sell Your First Private-Label Product*

- **FOREX Trading**: *A Simplified Guide To Maximizing Profits, Minimizing Losses and How to Use Fundamental Analysis & Trading Techniques to Thrive in a Bear and Bull Market*